THE HEALTHY KITCHEN

SUGAR FREE

hinkler

CONTENTS

hinkler

Published by Hinkler Books Pty Ltd
45–55 Fairchild Street
Heatherton Victoria 3202 Australia
www.hinkler.com.au

Design © Hinkler Books Pty Ltd 2015
Food photography and recipe development
© Stockfood, The Food Media Agency
Front cover image © Shutterstock.com: Ice-cream
with raspberries in glass bowl © Africa Studio
Typesetting: MPS Limited
Prepress: Graphic Print Group

ISBN: 978 1 7436 7732 2

Printed and bound in China

SUGAR FREE

Following a sugar-free diet can improve your health and reduce your chance of getting diabetes or becoming overweight. Cutting sugar from your diet has other important benefits.

- Sugar cravings are drastically reduced.
- You don't feel hungry so as often.
- Fatigue is significantly reduced.
- You have a clearer, more focused mental state.
- You feel more energised and your skin looks better.

The body quickly metabolises sugar into blood sugar, triggering the release of insulin. Insulin surges promote fat storage. Research shows that every 1 gram of sugar eaten is converted into 2 grams of body fat. Eliminating sugar frees you from blood sugar highs and lows, and as your blood sugar stabilises, you don't experience energy highs or lows.

This book is packed with recipes for delicious sugar-free meals using nutritious whole foods, such as lentils, quinoa and barley; beneficial fats like olive oil; and non-starchy vegetables, such as onions, mushrooms and broccoli. Starchy vegetables, such as sweet potatoes, are included because they are necessary for nutrition but won't raise your blood sugar. They are also low on the glycaemic index (GI).

Low-GI foods raise blood sugar slowly, while high-GI foods can cause a 'sugar rush', affecting mood and increasing appetite. Low-GI foods, like oats, keep blood sugar levels steady, help your body metabolise fat more efficiently and make you feel fuller for longer.

Foods to avoid on a sugar-free diet include sucrose (table sugar), fructose (fruit sugar), maple syrup, corn syrup, palm sugar and brown sugar. These all contribute to weight gain and tooth decay and have no nutritional benefit. Processed foods are packed with hidden sugars and should also be avoided.

Although you shouldn't eat too much fruit, it's not wise to cut fruit from your diet altogether. One to two portions each day is ideal. Fruit provides fibre, vitamins and minerals, which are necessary for health. Where possible, our recipes use low-sugar fruits, such as apricots, berries and limes, which are crammed with antioxidants, amino acids and essential fatty acids. Some of our recipes use fruits that are higher in sugar, such as apples, cherries and pomegranates. However, the health benefits of consuming small amounts of these fruits outweigh their sugar content.

The sweet recipes also use two naturally sweet alternatives – stevia and rice malt syrup.

Stevia is a plant, grown mainly in South America and Asia. The dried leaves are steeped and the sweet compounds extracted. The extracts are about 300 times sweeter than sugar. Stevia contains no calories, no carbohydrates and doesn't raise blood sugar levels. It remains stable at high temperatures so is useful in baking and cooking.

Rice malt syrup – made from brown rice – is virtually fructose-free. It contains complex sugars, maltose (malt sugar) and a small amount of glucose. Glucose enters the bloodstream almost immediately, while maltose takes up to 90 minutes to digest. Coeliacs should check the label when buying rice syrup, as some brands include barley malt, which contains gluten.

BREAKFAST

For a refreshing start to the day, choose a breakfast that doesn't come out of a box. These creative recipes use wholesome ingredients that will give you a sugar-free energy boost.

PANCAKES WITH BLUEBERRIES AND CREAM CHEESE

Serves 4
Preparation and cooking 25 minutes

Ingredients:

180 g | 6 oz | 1½ cups plain (all-purpose) flour
½ tsp salt
1¾ tsp baking powder
3 eggs
3 tbsp melted butter
400 ml | 14 fl oz | 1⅔ cups milk
¼ tsp stevia
vegetable oil, for frying

To serve:
225 ml | 8 fl oz | 1 cup low-fat cream cheese (quark)
150 g | 5 oz | 1½ cups blueberries

Method:

1. Sift the flour, salt and baking powder into a mixing bowl.

2. Beat together the eggs, butter, milk and stevia until well combined.

3. Add the liquid mixture to the dry ingredients and mix until just combined. Do not over-mix.

4. Heat a little oil in a frying pan (skillet) and ladle portions of the batter into the pan.

5. Cook for about 1–2 minutes, until bubbles appear on the surface, then turn over and cook the other side until lightly golden.

6. Stir together the low-fat cream cheese (quark) and blueberries, crushing the berries lightly. Serve with the pancakes.

BREAKFAST OAT BARS

Makes 8–9 bars
Preparation and cooking 30 minutes

Ingredients:

200 g | 7 oz | 2 cups rolled oats, plus extra for sprinkling
25 g | 1 oz | ⅓ cup desiccated (fine) coconut
170 ml | 6 fl oz | ¾ cup rice malt syrup, warmed
30 ml | 1 fl oz | ⅛ cup melted coconut oil

Method:

1. Heat the oven to 180°C (160°C fan | 350°F | gas 4). Grease a 20 cm | 8" square tin.

2. Mix together all the ingredients until well blended.

3. Press the mixture into the tin and smooth the top. Sprinkle with rolled oats.

4. Bake for about 20 minutes, until golden. Cool completely in the tin, then cut into bars.

BREAKFAST EGG TARTS

Makes 6 tarts
Preparation and cooking 1 hour + chilling 30 minutes

Ingredients:

For the pastry:
200 g | 7 oz | 1¾ cups plain (all-purpose) flour, plus
    extra for dusting
½ tsp salt
100 g | 3½ oz | ½ cup butter
1 egg, beaten
2 tbsp water

For the filling:
110 g | 4 oz cooked ham, cut into strips
2 tbsp chopped spring (green) onions, green part only
½ small red capsicum (pepper), finely chopped
12 small eggs, or 6 medium eggs
2 tbsp double (heavy, 48% fat) cream
25 g | 1 oz | ¼ cup grated parmesan cheese
salt
freshly ground black pepper

Method:

1. For the pastry: sift the flour into a mixing bowl and stir in the salt. Rub in the butter until the mixture resembles breadcrumbs. Gradually add the egg and water, a tablespoon at a time, mixing continuously until the mixture just comes together as a dough. (You may not need to use all the water.) Roll the dough into a ball, then wrap in cling wrap (plastic film) and chill for 30 minutes.

2. Heat the oven to 200°C (180°C fan | 400°F | gas 6). Grease 6 tart tins, 10 cm | 4" diameter.

3. Roll out the dough on floured surface and line the tins. Prick the base of the pastry case several times with a fork.

4. Cover the pastry with a sheet of non-stick baking paper and fill it with rice or dried beans. Bake for 10 minutes, until the pastry is pale golden. Remove from the oven, discard the beans and paper and bake for a further 5 minutes. Set aside to cool.

5. For the filling: line the bottom of each pastry case with the ham and sprinkle with spring (green) onions and red capsicum (pepper).

6. Crack 1 or 2 eggs into the centre. Pour 1 teaspoon of cream over each egg and sprinkle with 2 teaspoons of cheese.

7. Bake for about 15 minutes, until the whites are set and the yolks are cooked. Sprinkle with salt and pepper.

SCRAMBLED EGGS WITH PEPPERS

Serves 4
Preparation and cooking 20 minutes

Ingredients:

25 g | 1 oz | ⅛ cup butter
1 green capsicum (pepper), seeds removed, chopped
1 onion, chopped
bacon slices
4 large eggs
3–4 tbsp milk
1 pinch salt
freshly ground pepper

Method:

1. Heat the butter in a shallow pan and cook the capsicum (pepper) and onion until soft, but not browned.

2. Heat the grill and cook the bacon on both sides until cooked to your liking.

3. Beat together the eggs, milk and salt and stir into the pan.

4. Stir over a low heat until the scrambled eggs are cooked through, but still light and fluffy. Season with salt and pepper and serve immediately with bacon.

SPICY CHEESE MUFFINS

Makes 12 muffins
Preparation and cooking 50 minutes

Ingredients:

300 g | 11 oz | 2½ cups self-raising flour
150 g | 5 oz | 1½ cups rolled oats
1½ tsp English mustard powder
1 tsp baking powder
½ tsp bicarbonate of (baking) soda
350 g | 12 oz zucchini (courgettes), grated and drained
300 g | 11 oz | 2½ cups grated strong cheddar (American) cheese
175 ml | 6 fl oz | ¾ cup milk
2 eggs
10 tbsp sunflower oil
8–9 tbsp pine nuts

Method:

1. Heat the oven to 180°C (160°C fan | 350°F | gas 4). Place paper cases or liners in 12 muffin tins.

2. Sift the dry ingredients into a mixing bowl and add the grated zucchini (courgettes) and cheese.

3. Whisk together the milk, egg and oil and add to the bowl. Gently stir the wet ingredients into the dry until just combined.

4. Spoon into the tins and sprinkle with pine nuts. Bake for about 25 minutes, until risen and golden. Serve warm.

SAUSAGE BREAKFAST BAKE

Serves 4
Preparation and cooking 55 minutes

Ingredients:

5 tbsp olive oil
450 g | 16 oz sausages, cut into chunks
2 large potatoes, peeled and thickly sliced
1 green capsicum (pepper), seeds removed, sliced
1 yellow capsicum (pepper), seeds removed, sliced
1 onion, cut into wedges
125 ml | 4½ fl oz | ½ cup vegetable stock (broth)
salt and pepper, to taste
4 eggs
2 tsp mixed dried herbs

Method:

1. Heat the oven to 190°C (170°C fan | 375°F | gas 5).

2. Heat 1 tablespoon of oil in a frying pan (skillet) and brown the sausages. Place in a baking tin.

3. Heat the remaining oil in the frying pan and cook the potatoes, stirring occasionally, until browned. Place the potatoes in the baking tin.

4. Add the capsicums (peppers) and onion to the frying pan and cook for 5 minutes, until beginning to soften. Place in the baking tin.

5. Pour the stock (broth) over the vegetables and sausage and season with salt and pepper. Gently stir the sausage, potatoes and vegetables together.

6. Bake for 20–25 minutes, cracking in the eggs and sprinkling with the mixed dried herbs for the last 5–10 minutes, until the eggs are cooked to your liking.

CREAMY OATS

Serves 4
Preparation and cooking 15 minutes

Ingredients:

200 g | 7 oz | 2 cups rolled oats
1 l | 35 fl oz | 4 cups milk
1 pinch salt
2–3 tbsp rice malt syrup

To serve:
1 red apple, grated
raspberries
blueberries
pumpkin seeds
sunflower seeds
sultanas (golden raisins) (optional)

Method:

1. Put the oats, milk, salt and rice malt syrup (to taste) into a pan. Bring to a boil, stirring constantly, then simmer gently for 4–6 minutes until creamy.

2. Put into serving bowls, stir in the apple, sprinkle with seeds and place the berries and sultanas (golden raisins) on top.

FRITTERS WITH SMOKED SALMON AND POACHED EGGS

Serves 4
Preparation and cooking 25 minutes

Ingredients:

3 zucchinis (courgettes), coarsely grated and drained
1 onion, finely chopped
1 large egg, beaten
55 g | 2 oz | ½ cup plain (all-purpose) flour
3 tbsp grated parmesan cheese
salt
freshly ground black pepper
vegetable oil, for frying

For the poached eggs:
1 tbsp vinegar
4 eggs

To serve:
smoked salmon slices

To garnish:
salad cress (watercress)

Method:

1. Mix together the zucchinis (courgettes) and onion in a bowl.

2. Mix together the egg, flour and cheese. Stir into the zucchini mixture. Season with salt and pepper to taste.

3. Heat the oil in a large frying pan (skillet) over a medium heat. Drop large tablespoons of the mixture in the pan and cook for 2–3 minutes on each side until crisp and golden brown. Drain on absorbent kitchen paper.

4. For the poached eggs: heat about 4 cm | 2" of water in a frying pan to a simmer. Add the vinegar. Gently crack the eggs into a small bowl and slide them into the simmering water. Poach the eggs for 3–4 minutes, until just set.

5. Place the fritters on serving plates and top with smoked salmon and poached eggs. Sprinkle with black pepper and garnish with salad cress (watercress).

LUNCH

These healthy lunch recipes are a great way to increase your vegetable intake. There are hearty lunches for the cooler months, lighter lunches for the warmer months and options that work well all year round.

STUFFED SWEET POTATOES

Serves 4
Preparation and cooking 45 minutes

Ingredients:

4 sweet potatoes (yams), approx. 300 g | 11 oz each
olive oil
8 sundried tomatoes, in oil, drained, oil reserved, roughly chopped
1–2 cloves garlic, crushed
50 g | 1¾ oz black (ripe) olives, pitted, finely chopped
200 g | 7 oz sheep's or goat's cheese, diced
1 tbsp lemon juice
salt
freshly ground black pepper

Method:

1. Heat the oven to 220°C (200°C fan | 425°F | gas 7).

2. Rub the sweet potatoes (yams) all over with olive oil and wrap in pieces of non-stick baking paper, tying the ends with kitchen string.

3. Place on a baking tray (sheet) or in a roasting tin and bake in the oven for about 25 minutes until tender.

4. Mix together the tomatoes, garlic, olives, cheese and 2 tablespoons of the oil from the sundried tomatoes. Season with lemon juice, salt and ground black pepper.

5. Carefully open the parcels and slit the potatoes lengthways. Gently pull open and spoon in the filling. Bake for a further 10 minutes to brown the cheese.

6. If desired, serve in the baking paper for a rustic touch.

QUINOA SALAD WITH POMEGRANATE SEEDS

Serves 4
Preparation and cooking 40 minutes

Ingredients:

200 g | 7 oz | 1 cup (heaped) quinoa
4 tbsp olive oil
4 sweet potatoes (yams), peeled and cubed
1 head broccoli, broken into florets (flowerets)
1 handful baby spinach
2 limes, juice
2–4 tbsp extra virgin olive oil
salt and pepper

To garnish:
1 pomegranate, seeds
sunflower seeds
Greek yoghurt

Method:

1. Cook the quinoa according to the packet instructions. Drain, rinse and set aside.

2. Heat the oil in a pan and gently cook the sweet potatoes (yams), stirring from time to time, for about 8 minutes until tender.

3. Cook the broccoli in a pan of boiling salted water until tender. Drain and refresh in cold water, then drain again.

4. Fluff the quinoa gently with a fork and put into a bowl.

5. Whisk together the lime juice, olive oil and a pinch of salt and add to the quinoa with the vegetables. Stir gently to combine. Season to taste with salt and pepper.

6. Place on a serving plate and sprinkle with pomegranate and sunflower seeds. Drizzle with yoghurt.

ASIAN CHICKEN SALAD WITH NOODLES

Serves 4
Preparation and cooking 25 minutes

Ingredients:

225 g | 8 oz rice noodles
1 tbsp vegetable oil
1 cm | ½ in piece ginger (gingerroot), sliced
2 carrots, very thinly sliced
20 baby corn cobs
2 tbsp light soy sauce
1 tbsp lime juice
1 tbsp sesame oil
350 g | 12 oz cooked chicken, sliced
100 g | 3½ oz | 1 cup bean sprouts
4 spring (green) onions, thinly sliced
salt and pepper

To garnish:
coriander (cilantro) leaves
lime wedges
roasted peanuts, chopped

Method:

1. Place the rice noodles in a large bowl and cover with boiling water. Leave to stand for 3–5 minutes, or according to the packet instructions. When the noodles are just tender, drain thoroughly and return to the bowl.

2. Heat a wok over high heat and add the oil. When the oil starts to smoke, add the ginger (gingerroot) slices and stir-fry (scramble-fry) for a few seconds. Add the carrots and corn cobs with a small splash of water and cook for a further 5 minutes, until tender but still a little crunchy. Season to taste with salt and put into the bowl.

3. Mix together the soy sauce, lime juice and sesame oil. Add to the noodles with the chicken, bean sprouts and spring (green) onions. Season to taste and toss together to mix.

4. Garnish with coriander (cilantro) and lime wedges and serve with peanuts.

BARLEY CAKES

Serves 4–6
Preparation and cooking 1 hour 10 minutes + chilling 30 minutes

Ingredients:

2 sticks celery, chopped
4 spring (green) onions, chopped
2 cloves garlic
2 bay leaves
1 tsp chopped thyme
300 g | 11 oz | 1½ cups pearl barley
675 ml | 24 fl oz | 3 cups vegetable stock (broth)
½ teaspoon salt
freshly ground pepper
olive oil

To serve:
beetroot (beet), cut into julienne strips
salad leaves

Method:

1. Put the celery, spring (green) onions, garlic, herbs, barley and stock (broth) in a pan and bring to a boil, stirring constantly. Cover and simmer very gently for about 30 minutes, until all the stock is absorbed. Remove the bay leaves.

2. Remove from the heat, season with salt and pepper and put half the mixture in a blender or food processor and blend to a puree.

3. Stir the puree into the remaining barley mixture. Leave to cool and chill until firm.

4. Heat the oven to 200°C (180°C fan | 400°F | gas 6). Grease a baking tray (sheet).

5. Shape the mixture into patties with damp hands.

6. Place on the baking tray and brush with oil. Bake for 15–20 minutes until lightly golden.

7. Serve with salad and julienned beetroot (beet).

SWEET POTATO SOUP

Serves 4
Preparation and cooking 1 hour

Ingredients:

3 tbsp olive oil
2 onions, chopped
5 cm | 2" piece ginger (gingerroot), finely chopped
1 clove garlic, finely chopped
4 sweet potatoes (yams), peeled and chopped
1 l | 35 fl oz | 4 cups vegetable stock (broth)
200 g | 7 oz | ⅞ cup crème fraîche
salt
freshly ground black pepper
grated nutmeg

To garnish:
crème fraîche
½ cabbage, leaves shredded
toasted pecan nuts

Method:

1. Heat the oil in a large pan and cook the onions until starting to soften.

2. Add the ginger (gingerroot) and garlic and cook for a further 2–3 minutes.

3. Add the sweet potatoes (yams) and cook for a further 10 minutes, stirring occasionally.

4. Stir in the stock (broth), cover and simmer very gently for about 25 minutes, until the sweet potato is tender. Cool slightly.

5. Transfer the soup in batches to a blender or food processor and blend until smooth.

6. Return to the pan and add the crème fraîche. Season to taste with salt, pepper and nutmeg.

7. Put the cabbage in a pan and add just enough boiling water to cover. Cover and cook for 3–4 minutes until wilted. Drain well.

8. Reheat gently and serve garnished with a swirl of crème fraîche, cooked cabbage and pecan nuts.

LENTIL SALAD WITH SMOKED TROUT

Serves 4
Preparation and cooking 50 minutes

Ingredients:

2 tbsp olive oil

1 stick celery, chopped

3 carrots, diced

1 zucchini (courgette), chopped

225 g | 8 oz | 1 cup puy (green) lentils

1 bouquet garni, fresh or dried

2 tbsp balsamic vinegar

6 tbsp extra virgin olive oil

salt

freshly ground black pepper

4 spring (green) onions, chopped

4 smoked trout fillets

To garnish:

pea shoots or watercress

Method:

1. Heat the olive oil in a frying pan (skillet) and cook the celery, carrots and zucchini (courgette) over a low heat until tender but not browned. Remove from the pan and set aside.

2. Put the lentils in a pan with the bouquet garni. Cover with water and bring to a boil. Cover and simmer for 25 minutes. Leave to stand for 5 minutes, until the water is almost completely absorbed.

3. Remove the bouquet garni and tip the lentils into a bowl.

4. Whisk together the vinegar and extra virgin olive oil. Season to taste with salt and pepper.

5. Add the dressing to the warm lentils, with the celery, carrots, zucchini and spring (green) onions, mixing well. Leave to become cold, then divide between 4 serving plates.

6. Place the trout fillets on top and garnish with pea shoots or watercress.

Tip: A bouquet garni is a bundle of herbs, such as bay leaves, parsley and thyme, tied together with string. Dried bouquet garni can also be found at most supermarkets.

BEEF WRAPS

Serves 4
Preparation and cooking 20 minutes

Ingredients:

4 soft flour tortillas
4–5 tbsp hummus
lettuce or spinach leaves
½ red onion, thinly sliced
1 firm tomato, diced
4 slices roast beef
salt and pepper
coriander (cilantro) leaves

To serve:
diced tomatoes
chopped basil
potato chips (crisps)

Method:

1. Spread the tortillas with the hummus.

2. Lay the lettuce or spinach leaves on top.

3. Divide the onion and tomato between the wraps and place a slice of beef on each wrap. Season to taste with salt and pepper.

4. Place a few coriander (cilantro) leaves on each wrap. Roll up the wraps and cut each into 2–3 pieces.

5. Serve with a bowl of diced tomatoes sprinkled with basil and potato crisps.

THAI BEEF SALAD

Serves 4
Preparation and cooking 25 minutes

Ingredients:

250 g | 9 oz rice noodles
500 g | 18 oz sirloin steak
sesame oil
salt and pepper
1 tbsp fish sauce
1 tbsp lime juice
1 cucumber, seeds removed, chopped
200 g | 7 oz cherry tomatoes, halved
6–8 cooked baby carrots
2–3 tbsp Thai basil leaves
2–3 tbsp mint leaves
2–3 tbsp coriander (cilantro) leaves
1 long red chilli, seeds removed, thinly sliced

To garnish:
shaved coconut
4–5 tbsp roasted peanuts

Method:

1. Heat the grill.

2. Place the rice noodles in a large bowl and cover with boiling water. Leave to stand for 3–5 minutes, or according to the packet instructions. When the noodles are just tender, drain thoroughly and return to the bowl.

3. Brush both sides of the steak with oil and season well with salt and pepper. Grill for 3–4 minutes on each side or until cooked to your liking. Transfer to a plate and loosely cover with foil. Set aside for 5 minutes to rest.

4. Whisk together the fish sauce and lime juice.

5. Place the noodles, cucumber, tomatoes, carrots, basil, mint, coriander (cilantro) and chilli in a bowl. Drizzle with dressing and gently toss until just combined.

6. Thinly slice the beef and add to the salad. Gently toss until just combined. Divide among serving bowls and garnish with shaved coconut and sprinkle with peanuts.

DINNER

Try these recipes for healthy dinners that are full of colour, flavour and nutritious ingredients. They are easy to prepare for everyday dinners but impressive enough for entertaining.

BEEF AND ALE STEW

Serves 4
Preparation and cooking 3 hours 25 minutes

Ingredients:

3 tbsp olive oil
750 g | 26 oz stewing beef, cut into 3 cm | 1½" pieces
2 onions, coarsely chopped
1 clove garlic, crushed
4 carrots, coarsely chopped
1 tbsp flour
1 tsp ground allspice
1 tbsp tomato paste (puree)
salt and pepper
400 ml | 14 fl oz | 1⅔ cups beef stock (broth)
200 ml | 7 fl oz | ⅞ cup ale
2 bay leaves

To garnish:
flat-leaf parsley
thyme

Method:

1. Heat the oven to 160°C (140°C fan | 325°F | gas 3).

2. Heat the oil in a flameproof casserole dish or large pan and add the meat in batches. Fry quickly until brown on all sides. Remove the meat and set aside.

3. Add the chopped onions, garlic and carrots to the fat left in the casserole dish and cook for a few minutes until lightly browned.

4. Add the flour, allspice, tomato paste (puree), salt and pepper and cook for 1 minute, stirring, then add the beef stock (broth), ale and bay leaves.

5. Bring to a boil, stirring constantly. Add the meat and cover the casserole dish. If using a pan, put into a deep baking dish.

6. Transfer to the oven and cook for 2–3 hours, until the meat is very tender but not stringy. Garnish with parsley and thyme.

SPAGHETTI WITH FETTA, OLIVES AND SUNDRIED TOMATOES

Serves 4
Preparation and cooking 35 minutes

Ingredients:

375 g | 13 oz wholemeal (wholewheat) spaghetti
16–20 black (ripe) olives, pitted and halved
10 sundried tomatoes in oil, drained, roughly chopped
200 g | 7 oz fetta cheese

To garnish:
rocket (arugula)

For the dressing:
4 tbsp oil, from the sundried tomatoes
1½ tbsp balsamic vinegar
1 tsp chopped oregano
salt
freshly ground black pepper

Method:

1. Cook the spaghetti in a pan of salted boiling water, according to the packet directions until al dente. Drain and return to the pan.

2. For the dressing: whisk together all the ingredients and stir half the mixture into the hot spaghetti.

3. Tip the spaghetti into a bowl and add the olives and tomatoes, mixing well. Add the remaining dressing and toss to mix.

4. Divide between 4 serving plates and crumble over the cheese. Garnish with rocket (arugula).

BARLEY RISOTTO WITH MUSHROOMS

Serves 4
Preparation and cooking 55 minutes

Ingredients:

4 tbsp olive oil

500 g | 18 oz mixed mushrooms, e. g. enoki, shiitake, porcini, oyster; large mushrooms should be chopped

1 onion, finely diced

250 g | 9 oz | 1¼ cups pearl barley

1 bay leaf

2–3 sprigs thyme, leaves picked, reserving one sprig whole for garnish

120 ml | 4 fl oz | ½ cup dry white wine

800 ml | 28 fl oz | 3½ cups vegetable stock (broth)

½ unwaxed orange, juice and zest

100 g | 3½ oz | 1 cup grated pecorino cheese

salt

freshly ground black pepper

Method:

1. Heat half the oil in a pan and fry the mushrooms for 5 minutes. Remove from the pan.

2. Heat the remaining oil and cook the onion until softened. Add the pearl barley, bay leaf and thyme leaves and fry for 2 minutes.

3. Deglaze with the wine and allow to evaporate, then pour in the stock (broth). Simmer for 20–30 minutes until the barley is soft but still has a little bite. Add water if it becomes too dry.

4. Stir in the mushrooms, orange juice and zest and half the cheese.

5. Season to taste with salt and ground black pepper then place on warm serving plates. Serve garnished with thyme and the remaining cheese.

SALMON AND VEGETABLE BAKE

Serves 4
Preparation and cooking 1 hour 20 minutes

Ingredients:

4 salmon fillets
2 tbsp olive oil
4–6 zucchinis (courgettes), sliced
2 cloves garlic, finely chopped
4 spring (green) onions, sliced
1 head broccoli, broken into florets (flowerets)
300 g | 11 oz plain yoghurt
1 egg
1 tbsp dijon mustard
½ unwaxed lemon, grated zest and juice
50 g | 1¾ oz | ½ cup grated cheese
2 tbsp snipped chives

Method:

1. Heat the oven to 200°C (180°C fan | 400°F | gas 6). Grease a baking dish.

2. Place the salmon in a shallow pan and pour over enough cold water to cover. Bring to a boil then reduce the heat and poach gently for 10–12 minutes until just cooked through. Remove from the cooking liquid and flake the flesh.

3. Heat the oil in a large frying pan (skillet), then add the zucchinis (courgettes), garlic and spring (green) onions and cook, stirring occasionally, for 5–7 minutes, until the zucchinis begin to soften. Remove from the heat.

4. Steam the broccoli florets (flowerets) for 4–5 minutes until just tender. Chop the florets roughly.

5. Layer the zucchini mixture, broccoli and salmon in the baking dish.

6. Whisk together the yoghurt, egg, mustard, lemon zest and juice, season to taste and spoon over the broccoli and salmon to coat.

7. Bake for about 20 minutes until piping hot. Sprinkle with cheese and chives for the last 5 minutes of cooking time.

LAMB CUTLETS WITH A HARISSA CRUST

Serves 4
Preparation and cooking 1 hour

Ingredients:

3 tsp harissa paste
50 g | 1¾ oz | 1 cup fresh breadcrumbs
1 tbsp chopped coriander (cilantro)
4 lamb cutlets
5 tbsp olive oil
3 onions, sliced
2 cloves garlic, crushed
2 bay leaves
4 red capsicums (peppers), seeds removed and cut into strips
2 yellow capsicums (peppers), seeds removed and cut into strips
200 g | 7 oz ripe tomatoes, chopped
salt
freshly ground pepper
15–20 black (ripe) olives, pitted
1 tbsp torn basil
1 tsp chopped oregano
½ tbsp lemon juice

To garnish:
coriander
croutons

Method:

1. Mix together the harissa paste, breadcrumbs and coriander (cilantro). Spread over the fat sides of the lamb cutlets and season to taste.

2. Heat 1 tablespoon of oil in a frying pan (skillet) and cook the cutlets for 3–4 minutes on each side. Remove from the pan and keep warm.

3. Heat the remaining oil in a large frying pan over a medium heat. Add the onions, garlic and bay leaves and cook gently for 5 minutes, stirring occasionally.

4. Add the capsicums (peppers) to the pan, cover and cook gently for 10 minutes.

5. Add the tomatoes and season well with salt and pepper. Cook, uncovered, stirring frequently, for 30 minutes or until the mixture is thick.

6. Remove the bay leaves and stir in the olives, herbs and lemon juice.

7. Serve with the cutlets and garnish with coriander and croutons.

MOROCCAN TABBOULEH

Serves 4
Preparation and cooking 20 minutes + standing 25 minutes

Ingredients:

225 g | 8 oz cracked wheat
50 g | 1¾ oz parsley, finely chopped
8 spring (green) onions, finely chopped
4 tbsp lemon juice
1 tsp salt, plus more if desired
450 g | 16 oz cherry tomatoes, halved
40 g | 1½ oz mint leaves, finely chopped
½ cucumber, very finely chopped
4 tbsp extra virgin olive oil
freshly ground black pepper

To garnish:
coriander (cilantro) leaves

Method:

1. Put the cracked wheat in a bowl and cover with plenty of cold water. Leave to stand for 20–25 minutes, until the grains have softened.

2. Tip into a sieve lined with a tea towel and squeeze to extract as much water as possible.

3. Tip the wheat into a large bowl and stir in the parsley, spring (green) onions, lemon juice and salt until well mixed.

4. Add the tomatoes to the wheat mixture with the mint, cucumber and oil and mix well. Season to taste with salt and pepper.

5. Serve garnished with coriander (cilantro).

CHERMOULA CHICKEN WITH QUINOA SALAD

Serves 4
Preparation and cooking 45 minutes + marinating 1 hour

Ingredients:

2 cloves garlic, finely chopped
1 tsp ground cumin
1 tsp paprika
3 tbsp chopped parsley
3 tbsp chopped coriander (cilantro)
1 preserved lemon, finely chopped
2 tbsp lemon juice
2 tbsp olive oil
4 skinless boneless chicken breasts

For the quinoa salad:
50 g | 1¾ oz | ⅓ cup quinoa, rinsed
1 tbsp lemon juice
1 tsp extra-virgin olive oil
salt
freshly ground pepper
10 g | ⅓ oz | ¼ cup chopped fresh flat-leaf parsley leaves
1 small cucumber, thinly sliced
5–6 radishes, sliced
mint leaves

Method:

1. Whisk together all the ingredients, except the chicken, or blend to a paste in a food processor.

2. Put into a bowl and add the chicken. Coat the chicken on both sides in the mixture. Cover and marinate for at least 1 hour.

3. Heat the grill.

4. Cook the chicken for 5–7 minutes on each side until the chicken is cooked through, with no pink juices remaining when pierced with a knife.

5. For the quinoa salad: place the quinoa and 1 cup cold water in a pan over a high heat. Cover and bring to a boil. Reduce the heat and simmer for 10–12 minutes until the water is absorbed. Drain well and put into a large bowl.

6. Whisk together the lemon juice and oil. Season with salt and pepper. Add the remaining ingredients to the quinoa and toss to combine.

7. Serve the chicken warm or cold with quinoa salad.

FRESH RICE SALAD WITH COCONUT

Serves 4
Preparation and cooking 35 minutes + soaking 30 minutes + standing 10 minutes

Ingredients:

400 g | 14 oz | 2 cups basmati rice
1 tbsp vegetable oil
1 onion, chopped
1 red chilli, seeds removed, finely chopped (optional)
4 carrots, cut into sticks
2 red capsicums (peppers), seeds removed, cut into strips
100 g | 3½ oz bean sprouts
4 zucchinis (courgettes), sliced
3 tsp grated ginger (gingerroot)
2 cloves garlic, chopped
4 cardamom pods, lightly crushed
1 tsp ground cumin
675 ml | 24 fl oz | 3 cups vegetable stock (broth)
1 tsp salt
75 g | 2½ oz | ½ cup cashew nuts

To garnish:
sliced coconut
coriander (cilantro)

Method:

1. Rinse the rice in several changes of water to remove the excess starch, then soak in a bowl of cold water for 30 minutes. Drain well.

2. Heat the oil in a large pan and cook the onions, chilli, carrots and capsicum (pepper) strips for about 3–4 minutes until softened. Add the bean sprouts and zucchinis (courgettes) and cook for 2–3 minutes, stirring.

3. Add the ginger (gingerroot) and garlic and cook for 2 minutes. Stir in the spices and rice and cook for 1 minute until fragrant and the rice is coated.

4. Add the stock (broth) and salt and bring to a boil. Cover and simmer gently for about 10–15 minutes until the liquid is absorbed and vegetables are just tender, but still crisp. Leave to stand, covered, for 10 minutes until the rice is tender.

5. Toast the cashews in a dry frying pan (skillet) until lightly browned.

6. Stir the nuts into the rice mixture and put onto a warm serving plate.

7. Garnish with sliced coconut and coriander (cilantro).

DESSERT

Cutting down your sugar intake doesn't mean you have to deny yourself dessert. These delicious dessert recipes use low-sugar fruits, small amounts of higher-sugar fruits and sugar alternatives so you can still enjoy some sweetness in your life.

STRAWBERRY TART

Serves 6–8
Preparation and cooking 1 hour 15 minutes + chilling 1 hour 30 minutes

Ingredients:

For the pastry:
300 g | 11 oz | 2¾ cups plain (all-purpose) flour, plus extra for dusting
125 g | 4½ oz | ¾ cup ground almonds
1 pinch stevia
7 tbsp butter, diced
1 egg

For the filling:
570 ml | 20 fl oz | 2½ cups milk
1 pinch stevia
3 egg yolks
2 tbsp cornflour (cornstarch)
1 tsp vanilla extract
250–350 g | 9–12 oz strawberries
5 tbsp sugar-free strawberry jam (jelly) or spread
1 tbsp water

To decorate:
mint leaves

Method:

1. For the pastry: stir together the flour, ground almonds and stevia. Add the butter and egg and work to the consistency of breadcrumbs, then quickly knead into a dough. Wrap in cling wrap (plastic film) and chill for 30 minutes.

2. Heat the oven to 190°C (170°C fan | 375°F | gas 5). Lightly grease a 25 cm | 10" tart tin.

3. Roll out the chilled pastry on a lightly floured surface to 1 cm | ½" thickness and line the tin. Lay a piece of non-stick baking paper on top of the pastry and weigh it down with dried beans. Bake for 10–15 minutes until the base is dry. Remove from the oven and remove the beans and paper. Bake for a further 5–8 minutes until cooked through.

4. For the filling: heat the milk in a pan until warm. Stir in the stevia.

5. Whisk together the egg yolks, cornflour and vanilla. Stir in a little of the warm milk, then pour the mixture back into the pan. Cook, over a gentle heat, stirring until thickened. Remove from the heat and leave to cool, stirring from time to time.

6. Spoon the cooled custard onto the pastry base and chill until firm (approximately 1 hour). Arrange the strawberries on top.

7. Heat the jam (jelly) or spread and water until melted. Remove from the heat and allow to cool but not set.

8. Slowly drizzle the glaze over the strawberries and leave to set. Decorate with mint leaves.

VANILLA ICE-CREAM

Serves 4
Preparation and cooking 25 minutes + freezing 4 hours

Ingredients:

450 ml | 16 fl oz | 2 cups double (heavy, 48% fat) cream
1 vanilla pod (bean), seeds only
3 egg yolks
110 ml | 4 fl oz | 7 tbsp rice malt syrup

To serve:
raspberries
fresh mint

Method:

1. Heat the cream in a pan with the vanilla seeds until just boiling, then remove the pan from the heat and set aside.

2. Whisk the egg yolks with the rice malt syrup until fluffy, then gradually pour into the hot milk mixture, stirring all the time. Return the pan to a very gentle heat and cook, stirring continuously, until the mixture has thickened. Do not boil. Remove the pan from the heat, pour the custard into a clean bowl and leave to cool.

3. Pour into an ice-cream machine. Churn according to the manufacturer's instructions and freeze the ice-cream until ready to serve. Alternatively, pour into a freezerproof container and freeze for 4 hours, beating twice with a fork after each 2 hours, to break up any ice crystals, then cover and freeze until firm.

4. Serve with raspberries and fresh mint.

RASPBERRY TIRAMISU

Makes 9–12 pieces
Preparation and cooking 25 minutes + chilling 3 hours

Ingredients:

300 ml | 11 fl oz | 1⅓ cups cold espresso coffee
1–2 tbsp dark rum (optional)
30 sugar-free sponge fingers
1 unwaxed lemon, finely grated zest and juice
350 g | 12 oz | 1½ cups mascarpone
¼–½ tsp stevia, to taste
200 g | 7 oz sugar-free dark (semi-sweet) chocolate
375 g | 13 oz | 3 cups raspberries

Method:

1. Mix together the coffee and rum (if using). Line the base of a 20 cm | 8" square dish with half the sponge fingers. Brush the sponge fingers with half of the espresso coffee.

2. In a medium bowl, combine the lemon zest, lemon juice, mascarpone and stevia, mixing well to incorporate.

3. Carefully spread half of the mascarpone over the sponge fingers in the dish.

4. Coarsely grate half the chocolate and chop the rest into small chunks.

5. Sprinkle about two-thirds of the chocolate over the mascarpone and top with raspberries, reserving some raspberries for the top.

6. Arrange another layer of sponge fingers on top of the mascarpone and brush with the remaining espresso.

7. Spread with the remaining mascarpone and sprinkle with the remaining chocolate and raspberries. Chill for at least 3 hours before serving.

CHOCOLATE AND PEANUT-BUTTER CAKE

Makes 1 cake
Preparation and cooking 1 hour

Ingredients:

100 g | 3½ oz sugar-free dark (semi-sweet) chocolate, 70% cocoa solids, chopped
175 g | 6 oz | ¾ cup butter
3 large eggs
300 ml | 11 fl oz | 1⅓ cups rice malt syrup
120 g | 4 oz | 1 cup (heaped) plain (all-purpose) flour, plus 1 tbsp extra
¼ tsp bicarbonate of (baking) soda
2 tbsp cocoa or cacao powder
180 g | 6 oz | 1 cup peanut butter
2 tbsp roasted peanuts

Method:

1. Heat the oven to 180°C (160°C fan | 350°F | gas 4). Grease a 20–22 cm | 8"–9" cake tin and line the base with non-stick baking paper.

2. Melt the chocolate and butter in a heatproof bowl over a pan of simmering (not boiling) water. Remove from the heat.

3. Whisk together the eggs and rice malt syrup until very thick.

4. Whisk in the chocolate mixture until blended.

5. Sift in 120 g | 1 cup of flour, bicarbonate of (baking) soda and the cocoa and mix well. Mix the remaining flour with the peanut butter and peanuts and stir into the chocolate mixture.

6. Put into the tin and smooth the top. Bake for about 30 minutes until just firm. Cool completely in the tin.

COCONUT SLICE

Makes approx. 30 slices
Preparation and cooking 20 minutes + freezing 50 minutes

Ingredients:

225 g | 8 oz | 3 cups desiccated (fine) coconut, plus extra to decorate
150 g | 5 oz | ⅔ cup coconut oil
175 ml | 6 fl oz | ¾ cup coconut milk
1 tsp vanilla extract
½–1 tsp stevia
95 g | 3½ oz | ¾ cup raspberries

Method:

1. Grease a 15 cm x 25 cm | 6" x 10" tin and line the base with non-stick baking paper.

2. Put the desiccated (fine) coconut into a mixing bowl.

3. Heat the coconut oil, coconut milk, vanilla and stevia in a pan over a low heat and stir until melted and combined.

4. Remove from the heat and pour into the coconut. Mix well.

5. Press half the mixture into the tin and freeze until just firm (about 20 minutes).

6. Blend the raspberries to a puree, in a food processor until smooth. Press through a sieve into the remaining coconut mixture and mix well.

7. Press the pink mixture on top of the white mixture. Freeze for about 50 minutes until firm.

8. Sprinkle with coconut and cut into squares.

CARROT CAKE

Makes 1 cake
Preparation and cooking 1 hour 40 minutes

Ingredients:

2 eggs
75 ml | 2½ fl oz | ⅓ cup rice malt syrup
125 ml | 4½ fl oz | ½ cup sunflower oil
110 g | 4 oz | ⅞ cup wholemeal flour
110 g | 4 oz | 1 cup self-raising flour
1 tsp baking powder
1 tsp bicarbonate of (baking) soda
1 tsp ground cinnamon
1 tsp mixed spice
280 g | 10 oz | 5½ cups finely grated carrots
75 g | 2½ oz | ½ cup chopped walnuts
1 unwaxed orange, 1 tbsp juice and finely grated zest

For the topping:
250 g | 9 oz | 1 cup cream cheese
50 g | 1¾ oz | ¼ cup butter
1 tsp vanilla extract
rice malt syrup, to taste
75 g | 2½ oz | ½ cup chopped walnuts

Method:

1. Heat the oven to 170°C (150°C fan | 335°F | gas 3). Grease a deep 20 cm | 8" square cake tin and line the base with non-stick baking paper.

2. Separate 1 egg and put the yolk into a mixing bowl and the white into another bowl. Add the remaining whole egg to the yolk and add rice malt syrup. Whisk until thick and foamy.

3. Slowly pour in the oil and continue to whisk until well mixed. Sift in the dry ingredients and gently stir into the egg mixture until blended.

4. Whisk the egg white to soft peaks.

5. Fold the carrots, walnuts, orange juice and zest into the flour mixture. Gently fold in the whisked egg white until incorporated, then pour into the tin. Shake the tin to level the mixture.

6. Bake for about 1 hour until risen and firm and a skewer or wooden cocktail stick inserted in the centre comes out clean. Cool in the tin for 10 minutes, then place on a wire rack to cool completely.

7. For the topping: beat together all the ingredients except the walnuts until smooth. Spread on top of the cake and sprinkle with walnuts.

8. Cut into slices to serve.

RICE PUDDING WITH RHUBARB, VANILLA AND PINE NUTS

Serves 4
Preparation and cooking 55 minutes

Ingredients:

75 g | 2½ oz | ⅓ cup round-grain pudding rice
 (short-grained white rice)
900 ml | 32 fl oz | 4 cups milk
1 vanilla pod (bean), split down the centre
5–7 tbsp brown rice syrup
500 g | 18 oz rhubarb, cut into 5 cm | 2" lengths
100 ml | 3½ fl oz | 7 tbsp water

To decorate:
toasted pine nuts

Method:

1. Put the rice, milk and vanilla pod in a pan and bring to a simmer. Cook gently, stirring occasionally for 20–30 minutes, until the rice is cooked and creamy. Remove the vanilla pod.

2. Remove from the heat and add the 2–3 tablespoons of rice malt syrup, stirring well to incorporate.

3. Put the rhubarb, water and remaining rice malt syrup in a pan and bring to a simmer, stirring once or twice. Cook very gently until the rhubarb is tender but still holding its shape.

4. Spoon into serving dishes and divide the rice pudding between the dishes. Sprinkle with toasted pine nuts.

CHOCOLATE SOUFFLÉS

Serves 4–6
Preparation and cooking 50 minutes

Ingredients:

6 eggs, separated
2–3 pinches stevia, dissolved in 1 tbsp hot water
10 tbsp water
4 tbsp plain (all-purpose) flour
4 tbsp cocoa powder

Method:

1. Heat the oven to 180°C (160°C fan | 350°F | gas 4). Butter 4–6 soufflé dishes or individual ovenproof pudding basins.

2. Whisk the egg whites until stiff.

3. Whisk the egg yolks with the stevia mixture and water, then add the flour and cocoa and whisk until thick and creamy.

4. Gradually fold the egg whites into the mixture until combined.

5. Divide the mixture between the soufflé dishes and bake for 20–25 minutes, until risen and puffy. Serve immediately.

DRINKS

These drink recipes range from refreshing spritzers and punches to fruity and indulgent smoothies. Enjoy these blends of fresh ingredients and add a small amount of a sugar-free alternative if desired.

APPLE, AVOCADO AND GREEN-TEA SMOOTHIES

Serves 4
Preparation and cooking 20 minutes

Ingredients:

4 tsp matcha green-tea powder
2 tbsp hot water
1 large avocado, peeled, cut into chunks
1 large apple, sliced
225 g | 8 oz | 1 cup Greek yoghurt
300 ml | 11 fl oz | 1⅓ cups almond milk, more if needed
stevia, to taste

Method:

1. Whisk together the matcha powder and hot water. Set aside.

2. Put all the ingredients into a blender or food processor and blend until smooth. Add more milk if the mixture is too thick. Sweeten to taste. Chill before serving.

POMEGRANATE SPRITZERS

Serves 4
Preparation and cooking 25 minutes

Ingredients:

3 large pomegranates
ice
650–750 ml | 23–26 fl oz | 2⅔–3 cups sparkling water
stevia, to taste

To decorate:
lemon wedges

Method:

1. Cut the pomegranates in half and extract the seeds by tapping the skin of the pomegranate with a wooden spoon, ensuring the seeded side is held over a bowl.

2. Put seeds into chilled glasses, lightly crush and add the ice.

3. Top up with sparkling water. Sweeten to taste with stevia if desired.

4. Decorate with lemon wedges.

APRICOT, LAVENDER AND ALMOND SMOOTHIES

Serves 4
Preparation and cooking 15 minutes

Ingredients:

14 ripe apricots, pitted and halved
450 g | 16 oz | 2 cups plain yoghurt
225 ml | 8 fl oz | 1 cup almond milk
½ tsp dried culinary-grade lavender flowers

To decorate:
flaked toasted almonds

Method:

1. Put all the ingredients into a blender or food processor and blend until smooth. Chill before serving.

2. Pour into chilled glasses and sprinkle with flaked toasted almonds.

CHOCOLATE AND PEANUT SMOOTHIES

Serves 4
Preparation and cooking 15 minutes

Ingredients:

400 ml | 14 fl oz | 1⅔ cups almond or coconut milk, more if needed

4 tbsp peanut butter

6–8 tbsp raw cacao powder

1 tsp vanilla extract

½–1 tsp stevia

1 avocado, peeled and chopped

To decorate:

sugar-free grated chocolate

Method:

1. Put all the ingredients into a blender or food processor and blend until smooth and thick. Add more milk if desired.

2. Pour into chilled glasses and sprinkle with grated chocolate.

GREEN-TEA AND LIME PUNCH

Serves 4
Preparation and cooking 15 minutes + cooling 1 hour

Ingredients:

2 green-tea bags
500 ml | 18 fl oz | 2 cups water, heated to about 70°C
2 tbsp rice malt syrup
2 limes, juice
crushed ice

To garnish:
mint leaves
lime slices

Method:

1. Put the tea bags in the water and stir in the rice malt syrup.

2. Mix in the lime juice and let steep for 5 minutes.

3. Strain through a sieve and let it cool for 1 hour.

4. Pour the punch into glasses filled with crushed ice and garnish with the mint leaves and lime slices.

CHERRY AND CHOCOLATE SMOOTHIES

Serves 4
Preparation and cooking 15 minutes

Ingredients:

225 g | 8 oz | 1 cup pitted cherries
335 g | 12 oz | 1½ cups plain yoghurt
225 ml | 8 fl oz | 1 cup crushed ice
rice malt syrup, to taste

To decorate:
whipped (double) cream (optional)
cherries
grated sugar-free chocolate

Method:

1. Put all the ingredients into a blender or food processor and blend until smooth.

2. Pour into chilled glasses and top with whipped (double) cream, if desired. Sprinkle with grated chocolate and decorate with cherries.

COFFEE AND COCONUT SMOOTHIES

Serves 4
Preparation and cooking 15 minutes

Ingredients:

350 ml | 12 fl oz | 1½ cups coconut or almond milk

225 ml | 8 fl oz | 1 cup cold espresso coffee

110 g | 4 oz avocado, chopped

20–25 blanched almonds

stevia, to taste

110 ml | 4 fl oz | 7 tbsp crushed ice

To decorate:

cocoa powder

Method:

1. Put all the ingredients into a blender or food processor and blend until smooth.

2. Pour into chilled glasses and sprinkle with a little cocoa powder.

DETOX SMOOTHIES

Serves 4
Preparation and cooking 2 hours 15 minutes

Ingredients:

1 large globe artichoke, stem removed
175 g | 6 oz | 1¼ cups raspberries
100 ml | 3½ fl oz | 7 tbsp milk
200 g | 7 oz | ⅞ cup plain yoghurt
rice malt syrup, to taste

To decorate:
mint leaves

Method:

1. Put the artichoke into a pan of boiling water, cover and cook for 1 hour. Reduce the heat and simmer for 1 hour. Remove the artichoke (you won't need this). Set aside to cool completely.

2. Measure 200 ml | 1 cup of the artichoke liquid and put into a blender or food processor with the remaining ingredients. Blend until smooth. Chill before serving.

3. Pour into chilled glasses and decorate with mint leaves.

WEIGHTS AND MEASURES

Weights and measures differ from country to country, but with these handy conversion charts cooking has never been easier!

Weight Measures

Metric	Imperial
10 g	¼ oz
15 g	½ oz
20 g	¾ oz
30 g	1 oz
60 g	2 oz
115 g	4 oz (¼ lb)
125 g	4½ oz
145 g	5 oz
170 g	6 oz
185 g	6½ oz
200 g	7 oz
225 g	8 oz (½ lb)
300 g	10½ oz
330 g	11½ oz
370 g	13 oz
400 g	14 oz
425 g	15 oz
455 g	16 oz (1 lb)
500 g	17½ oz (1 lb 1½ oz)
600 g	21 oz (1 lb 5 oz)
650 g	23 oz (1 lb 7 oz)
750 g	26½ oz (1 lb 10½ oz)
1000 g (1 kg)	35 oz (2 lb 3 oz)

Cup Measurements

One cup of these commonly used sugar-free ingredients is equal to the following weights.

Ingredient	Metric	Imperial
Apples (dried and chopped)	125 g	4½ oz
Apricots (dried and chopped)	190 g	6¾ oz
Breadcrumbs (packet)	125 g	4½ oz
Breadcrumbs (soft)	55 g	2 oz
Butter	225 g	8 oz
Cheese (shredded/grated)	115 g	4 oz
Coconut (desiccated/fine)	90 g	3 oz
Flour (plain/all-purpose, self-raising)	115 g	4 oz
Fruit (dried)	170 g	6 oz
Margarine	225 g	8 oz
Nuts (chopped)	115 g	4 oz
Rice (cooked)	155 g	5½ oz
Rice (uncooked)	225 g	8 oz
Sugar-free choc bits	155 g	5½ oz

Liquid Measures

Cup	Metric	Imperial
¼ cup	63 ml	2¼ fl oz
½ cup	125 ml	4½ fl oz
¾ cup	188 ml	6⅔ fl oz
1 cup	250 ml	8¾ fl oz
1¾ cup	438 ml	15½ fl oz
2 cups	500 ml	17½ fl oz
4 cups	1 litre	35 fl oz

Spoon	Metric	Imperial
¼ teaspoon	1.25 ml	1/25 fl oz
½ teaspoon	2.5 ml	1/12 fl oz
1 teaspoon	5 ml	1/6 fl oz
1 tablespoon	15 ml	½ fl oz

Oven Temperatures

Celsius	Fahrenheit	Gas mark
120	250	1
150	300	2
160	320	3
180	350	4
190	375	5
200	400	6
220	430	7
230	450	8
250	480	9

INDEX